FIRST GRADE HISTORY

All About Christopher Columbus

BABY PROFESSOR

EDUCATION KIDS

Christopher Columbus was an explorer who's well known as the person who discovered America.

It was Columbus' voyage that started the exploration and colonization of the Americas.

Christopher Columbus
was born as
Cristofor Colombo in
Genoa Italy during
the year 1451.

His career in exploration started when he was very young. He studied geography and listened to stories from other sailors.

Columbus knew that there were great riches to be had in China and East Asia.

Christopher Columbus thought that if he traveled West he would find a shorter and easier route.

Columbus spent years
trying to convince
someone to pay
for his voyage.

In 1484 Columbus
asked King John
II of Portugal to
pay for his journey,
but the King was
not interested.

In 1492 King Ferdinand and his wife Queen Isabella decided to fund Columbus' trip and gave him ships and a crew.

He set sail on August 1492 with three ships named the Nina, the Pinta, and the Santa Maria.

During his first voyage in 1492, instead of arriving at Japan as he had intended, Columbus reached the New World.

It was a small island in the Bahamas that Columbus would name San Salvador.

Columbus thought
he had reached the
Indies so he called
the people Indians.

He also visited other islands in the Caribbean such as Cuba and Hispaniola.

After making
his discovery,
Columbus returned
home to Spain to
claim his riches.

On the way back
the Santa Maria
was shipwrecked on
Christmas Day in 1492
and never made the
trip back to Spain.

Columbus would make three more voyages to the Americas.

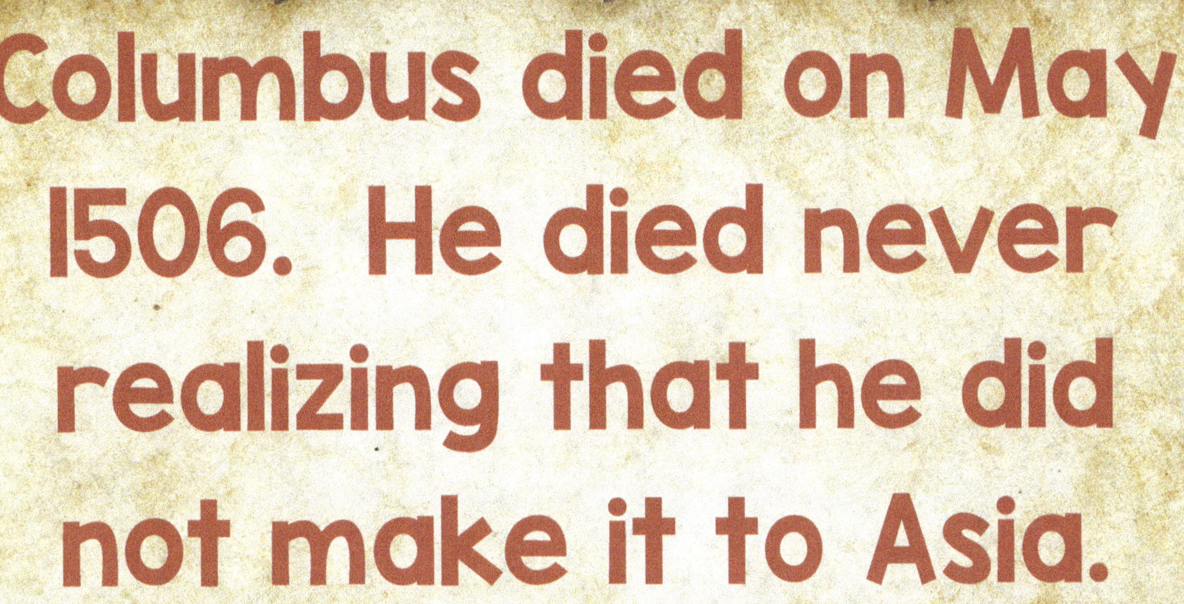

Columbus died on May 1506. He died never realizing that he did not make it to Asia.

Did you enjoy reading this book?
Share this to your friends.

Visit
BABY PROFESSOR
EDUCATION KIDS
www.BabyProfessorBooks.com
to download Free Baby Professor eBooks
and view our catalog of new and exciting
Children's Books